THE PAGES HAVEN'T RUN OUT YET

A Young Girl's Journey to Hope & Deliverance

GRACE GARNETT

The Pages Haven't Run Out Yet
Copyright © 2015 Grace Garnett

All rights reserved. No part of this book may be reproduced, distributed or transmitted in any form by any means, graphics, electronics, or mechanical, including photocopy, recording, taping, or by any information storage or retrieval system, without permission in writing from the publisher, except in the case of reprints in the context of reviews, quotes, or references.

Unless otherwise indicated, scripture quotations are from the New King James Version®. Copyright © 1982 by Thomas Nelson, Inc. All rights reserved.

Published by: Purposely Created Publishing Group™

Printed in the United States of America

ISBN: 1-942-83805-0
ISBN-13: 978-1-942838-05-0

Special discounts are available on bulk quantity purchases by book clubs, associations and special interest groups. For details email:
Sales@PublishYourGift.com or call (866) 674-3340.

For more information, log onto
www.PublishYourGift.com

Dedication

I would like to dedicate this book to my parents, Cassandra and Rodney, Sr.; my siblings, Richard, Rodney Jr., Joshua, Matrice, and Amina; my loving son, Jabriel; my grandmother, Nettie Johnson; the mother of rubies, Arnetta Whittaker; and my church family, New Gibeah Ministries for Christ.

Special shout out to my stepbrother, Marlon; my stepfathers, Joseph and Tracy; and my late grandmother, Joyce. To my spiritual father, Apostle Farmer, thank you for accepting me as your daughter. Even when I was broken and didn't believe in myself, you believed in me, loved me, and pushed me to be a mature woman of God.

And a special thank you to Tieshena Davis and Tarinna Terrell for helping me with my dreams and the vision God has for me.

Table of Contents

Dedication	iii
Introduction	vii
Deliverance Scriptures	ix
Chapter 1	1
Chapter 2	7
Chapter 3	13
Chapter 4	21
Chapter 5	29
Chapter 6	35
Chapter 7	41
Chapter 8	53
Conclusion	59
A New Journey	65
About the Author	69

Introduction

I never thought in a million years I'd be publishing this book. As a young girl, I started a journal as my way of releasing anger. The first few chapters of this book are actually derived from those same journals. I never knew that my story would be a testimony to save souls and bring people out of the darkness. A man of God, my awesome church leader and spiritual father helped to groom me into the mature woman of God that I was called to be. No matter what your situation may look like, no matter how hard it seems, if God blew breath into you to see another day, then He has purpose for you. You will get through it. I don't care what it is, you will come out of it because God loves you and He cares.

We have to go through a process. Much like being in your mother's womb, there are nine stages and you have to grow and develop through each stage. It's the same thing in the natural and spiritual realms. You have to keep growing until you grow into the person God called you to be. Never give up. Don't let your past stop you from becoming who you are called to be. God used me, and He *still* wants to use you.

When you read this, you will understand that the devil thought he had me, but God had a way out of darkness for me. I encourage anyone who's broken or has given up on life—if you're running from God because of church hurt or what people have done to you—to know that there is a God who stills loves you and has purpose for your life. No matter what you did or how big your sin is, God still wants to use you. Your past has been planted to build your purpose.

Deliverance Scriptures

Isaiah 38:17

Behold, for peace I had great bitterness: but thou hast in love to my soul delivered it from the pit of corruption: for thou hast cast all my sins behind thy back.

Isaiah 43:25

I, even I, am he that blotteth out thy transgressions for mine own sake, and will not remember thy sins.

1 Corinthians 1:27

But God hath chosen the foolish things of the world to confound the wise; and God hath chosen the weak things of the world to confound the things which are mighty;

One

I'd been searching for the light, but darkness continuously seemed to find me first. As a young girl finding love in all the wrong places, I never went too far. Could it be due to the fact that, at the age of two, my father was sent to jail for 15 years?

He was a pastor, a husband, and a father of five children. Before I was born, my father named me Grace, which means to be free. An oxymoron considering that my father was anything but free. He was in and out of the streets, doing drugs, and taking my mother's love for granted. Heartbreak was nothing new for my mother, especially abandonment. She lost her mother at the age of six, so marrying my father helped her heal some of the brokenness. She was closer to my father's side of the family. In fact, my paternal grandmother, Netty, was the first to take my mom to church. However, life didn't truly start until my father was sent to jail.

Growing up, my mother was a single mom of five kids. She worked hard, so she left our oldest brother in charge to watch the rest of us. Though she was away at work most of the time, she managed to always keep food on the table, clothes on our back, and a roof over our head. Yet, I still seemed to be unappreciative, never knowing why the anger continued to build up inside. I had heard stories about the time my father hit my mother, which made me angry. How was I expected to trust in God, or any man, for that matter? Sometimes my siblings and I were sent to our aunt's house. Her and my mother were very close to. Even though they were sister-in-laws, they were more like blood sisters. My aunt helped my mom when my father was sent to jail. So when my mom went to work, we went over to our aunt's house to be watched.

Of my mom's five kids, my brother and I gave her the most problems. We called each other "twins." He was my ride or die, and whenever I had a problem, I ran to him with it. We stayed in some type of trouble. Of all of our siblings, we were also the angriest ones. I fought every day in school just to prove my self-esteem. My mother eventually got fed up from having to move us from school to school due to our behavior and moved the family from DC to Maryland, hoping that me and my brother would behave better.

My grandmother was an elder and kept us in church as her way of teaching us how to behave. It didn't resolve the anger inside of me, however. Though our circumstances changed, my brother still had my back—good or bad! Though I considered my brother my twin and best friend, I never told a soul, not even my brother, that two family members had molested me at my aunt's house.

I was around seven or eight years old when I was told to come downstairs and lay across the bed. Imagine being told to shut up and to just lay there at seven years old, scared. Everyday my mother picked us up, I would run straight to my bed, asking God why. But it seemed like God never answered, so I'd end up crying myself to sleep. The sexual abuse went on for about five years. By the time I turned 12, I'd started fighting him off of me. One day, I got so mad that my anger overrode my fear of what he'd do to me, and I told my aunt what was happening. I wanted to tell my mother, but my aunt promised that she would tell her.

Weeks passed by and my mother still hadn't said anything to me about it, so I started hating her and doubting if anyone loved me. Deep down, I *knew* she loved me, but the thought that she could know what happened and still not say anything made me feel like she just didn't care. All she seemed to care about was work and her new man, after meeting him. Though he was a part of our lives, me and brother never accepted anyone, let alone him. My mother ended up pregnant with my baby sister, meaning my stepdad was playing an even bigger role than our biological father.

It didn't take long for me to start getting used to him being around though. I even started to call him dad. Though I was very careful about allowing another father figure in my life, my stepdad was actually doing a good job. About a year after my little sister was born, my mother and stepdad separated. Once again, my anger regained control.

As I got older, however, I learned how to get over childhood hurt—mainly through prayer and church.

Because my biological father was in prison, he never played a big part in my life. With my stepdad around, it didn't matter as much. When he left, it made me hate my father even more for not being there to protect me from all the hurt. I'd cry out his name when getting molested, yet he wasn't there to wipe my tears. I tried to face the fact that I didn't have a father, but that didn't make me feel any better. All I ever wanted to be was a daddy's girl. Like most girls seeking an absent father's love, I started looking for and finding love in all the wrong places.

Two

At the age of 14, I fell for the preacher's son. It was love at first sight. We locked eyes the entire service, and when it was over, he came over and gave me his number. After that day, we started seeing each other. He was my first boyfriend, and it felt like he was sent to heal all the brokenness, all the hurt, and all the pain. Little did I know, sometimes love can blind you.

We never had sex because I didn't allow anyone to touch me in that way. He didn't understand why I'd get so angry when he'd ask to have sex because I'd never told him that I'd been molested. Towards the middle of the relationship, he decided to try a little harder. He lived on the nice side of town in a mini mansion. One night, while his parents were gone, he invited me and my friend over. He started off kissing on me. That was fine, but when he started pushing himself on me, I shoved him away. He tried to hold the fact that we had been together for about a year over my head. None of his tactics worked though. And when I left that night, he blew my phone up, but I ignored his phone calls. The next day, he apologized, I forgave him, and we moved on. Weeks later, he asked again. Every time he'd ask, I'd say no. Eventually he stopped asking and didn't try again either.

Two years passed, and we were still dating. I'd never felt so safe in my life. Being with him made me feel like I was actually *living* again. He was my first love, or at least that's what I thought. Because I was kicked out of school, I wasn't able to go to prom or graduate from high school. So he took me to his prom. The day and night of the prom, I was happier than I had ever been in life. I just knew he was the one.

In the third year of our relationship, my twin brother came home with some bad news. The love of my life had a daughter on the way. He'd been cheating on me for months. That was my first real heartbreak, and no one could have prepared me for that feeling. After all, he was my first love, my first everything. My heart turned so cold that loving a man was *last* on my list of things to do. I didn't have my father, my stepdad walked out, and now my first love had broken my heart. Other than my brothers, men just couldn't be trusted.

I was even more angry and rebellious after that. I began sneaking out and running away from home in search of peace of mind. Because I'd gotten so out of control, my mother sent me off to Job Corp to get my GED. I took advantage of this newfound freedom by skipping school, smoking, drinking, and fighting. It was also during this time that I lost my virginity. Though he and I were dating, I was still scarred from my first boyfriend. Although he was very serious and committed to the relationship, I was only having fun. Like I said, falling in love was the last thing on my mind.

After two years of dating, I got pregnant and had a baby boy. Though we had a child, I still hadn't allowed myself to love again. Nor did I tell him about my past. It just all happened so fast. I met him at a party one day. He got my number. We would talk on the phone and, every now and then, he'd come see me or I'd skip school to go to see him. Then I was pregnant. It all happened so fast. I was 17 at this time. I'd gotten kicked out of Job Corp for skipping so much and had to move back in with my mom. That didn't last long though because my and my older sister moved out and got an apartment together. He moved in with us.

To an extent, I started falling in love with him. Having my son allowed me to love again. Plus, I didn't want my son to end up without his father like I did, so I tried my best to keep my little family together. For a minute, life was good. Then the thoughts came. Like I how I never really got over my first love. I realized that I was only dating my son's father, and had only hooked up with him in the first place, out of resentment and vengeance. My mind went downhill from there. Out of that same anger and bitterness, I'd lost my virginity, had my son, and was shacking up. Instead of moving forward, I had backtracked.

I started questioning if it was really love or lust. Confused, I started running the streets again.

By the time I realized that I didn't want to be in a relationship anymore, my son was one. I'd begun seeing other guys. I didn't want to keep hurting my son's father though, so I broke up with him. Because he was living with me and my sister, he had to leave. He fought for the family, but I just didn't want it. I didn't know how to be faithful or how to love because all my life I'd been broken. Being coldhearted was my nature. I'd gotten too used to lying and holding back on the truth.

All of the smoking, drinking, partying, and having sex started off fun. It made me feel free and in control of my own life. I was doing what I wanted to do with who I wanted to do it with. That life made me forget about all of my responsibilities and failures, and all of the hurt too. Problem was, I'd have fun at night, but then the regret would hit me the next day. That's when I'd miss my mom. Although I still had my issues with her, her spirit and her presence were comforting to me. I just wanted to be up under her. When I was with her, everything was okay.

Three

I felt so alone and unsupported, not realizing that my mother had my back all that time. I completely overlooked the fact that I actually had a really good, strong mother because I was so blind about the past. My mind couldn't see past the fact that my father wasn't there, my stepfather was no longer in the picture, my first love had betrayed me, all the remorse that had piled from nights of partying, and the fact that, after all those years, my mother still hadn't said nor done anything about me being molested. The issue continued to simmer inside of me.

The devil started to show up more and more in my life. The more I prayed and tried to find the light, the more darkness hovered. This is around the time that I started thinking about killing myself. Trusting God had always been a problem for me. I couldn't trust anyone, let alone someone who I couldn't even see. I tried getting closer to God, but my life in sin had a tighter grip on me. Fortunately, I maintained a good relationship with my son's grandmother. She started taking me to church. Though I didn't care much for her church, I did enjoy being back in the environment. So I started church hopping, trying to find one that I connected with.

I had a group of female friends that I'd grown up with. Before my father got locked up, he had a church with one of their father. We used to have one big house and lived together. When my father got arrested, we went our separate ways. We eventually reunited and picked up where we'd left off, treating each other like family. Lee Lee was my favorite of the group, so when one of her brothers died, I went to the funeral too. There, I met a pastor who spoke over my life. I was used to prophets because of my father's side of the family, but it was something different about that prophet. He moved my spirit in a way that I'd never experienced before. As he spoke to me, I felt love. Pure love. I asked him for the address to his church and from that day on, I wanted to go back to visit his church.

Me and my friends started visiting the church. After going for three weeks straight, I went ahead and joined. This congregation showed me so much love that I felt safe. While I desperately wanted to change my life, I still hadn't told anyone about my past and about the anger that resided in my heart. Trusting was still a difficult thing to do, but the more I stayed in the word, the better I was able to see the light. Within a year at the church, I'd confessed that Jesus died for our sins and rose on the third day. Now that I'd gotten saved and had given my life back to Christ, it seemed like my life got worse! Though I was learning, change doesn't happen overnight.

Two years into my membership at the church I'd learned how to better fight the devil and my flesh. The inner turmoil was still present, however. I'd crave the sin life, then I'd want Christ. I was genuinely confused. Feeling hopeless, I went back to what I knew which was finding love in all the wrong places. Unable to take any more heartbreak and pain, I'd cry every night. I'd fall to my knees praying to God that I'd find the light. Yet darkness continued to show its face. If it weren't for my son, I'd have given up.

Every time I thought of my baby boy, I'd want to do better for him. But I knew that I had to let go of the sin. One of my main prayers was for God to protect my son. I didn't want him to ever experience the things I did. Feeling like I had nowhere else to turn, I finally told someone at the church about all the anger that I was holding inside. That experience taught me that I could trust people more. I learned that I had to forgive or else I would never move on. But it seemed like after doing that, everything would get worse. There'd be a new distraction. In this case, it was another case of bad love. He had me over my head in love, doing things that I never thought I'd do like popping pills, smoking, drinking heavily, and hanging in the streets all hours of the night. Even though I was stuck in my dark ways, I always made sure that my son was in good hands, mainly with my mother.

Lee Lee was there for me when I needed to vent about him. Smoking and drinking was our way of releasing pain. There were times we would get off of work and head straight to the liquor store to get a drink. We would sit on her front porch some nights just to feel the summer air. While having long talks and laughter, we would get so drunk we'd start talking about him and his brother. Eventually we'd call them over and one thing would lead to another. Again, I would wake up regretting everything. I knew I was in a dark situation, and as crazy as it may sound, I loved it. Her house was my getaway from me and my sister's place. I would go there just so I could be with him. She was the only one who understood everything about me and him because she'd been there from the beginning. Plus, I told her everything about us. When he and I would get into it, I'd run straight to her.

A month later, he finally got a place with his brother, so I started to go over there every night. One day, we were out riding and his phone rang. I answered, and it was his baby mother, who I had no idea about. I handed him his phone, finding out she left when she was five months pregnant with his child, and now wanted to move back to DC to be with him. Needless to say, I was shocked! I had no idea he had a baby on the way. He explained everything to me, adding that he wasn't sure if the baby was his. Eventually, she ended up moving back to DC. I got fed up with all the drama and got back in the church. I kept seeing him, however. That is, until I found out that he was having sex with me, his child's mother, and another female. I declared that I'd never have sex with him again, refusing to allow myself to be a fool any longer. Bad enough, being with him had caused me to lose my job. Consequently, I couldn't help pay my rent or other bills.

We still maintained our bond though. We'd sit and tell each other secrets. I slowly began falling in love. In addition to the drugs, I did sexual things with him that I'd never done before. That's when I started realizing that the devil was taking over my life again. I found it in my heart to invite him to church with me. He came, but after that, he got worse! He started playing mind games, dealing with two different girls. I would cry nearly every night. As bad as I wanted out, it was hard to walk away.

I'd gotten myself stuck in a *soul tie*, which is when two people are joined together but aren't married. Because we were having sex, our souls were connected (or tied). Therefore, we were sharing energy. All of his negative energy and spirits became mine, and mine became his. The issues that I was already dealing with were made ten times worse, having to deal with his too—physically and spiritually. Soul ties are hard to break because emotions are involved. Instead of making rational decisions, you make emotional ones. Your emotions are in control of your flesh and soul. So even though I knew that I needed to leave, I couldn't.

As a soul tie would have it, every little thing he did bothered me. I began to get depressed, stressed, and having suicidal thoughts again. Back then I thought it was love. That was my emotions speaking. I'd also question that if it was love, why did I feel like I was dying? Letting him go was one of the most difficult decisions that I've ever made, but through prayer and a backbone, I finally found it in myself to walk away. I wish I'd known, however, that getting rid of him didn't end the soul tie.

So even after he left, I was still hurting. To make matters worse, my sister and I lost our apartment and had to move back in with our mother. No matter what we did or how much trouble we got in, our mother was always there. That wasn't enough for me though. So I'd go back around my old apartment to spend a night or two over at my partner in crime's house. We'd invite these two guys over and get drunk every night. After one particular wild night of drinking and partying, I ended up pregnant.

I'd never wanted to experience an abortion, but I had to get one. Not only was I not in the position to bring another child into the world, but there was absolutely no love involved between me and the father. I was terrified of telling my mother, but felt that I had no other choice since I was living under her roof. She didn't get mad though. In fact, she was very supportive of whichever decision I planned to make. For me, that meant getting an abortion. Although my reasons for doing so were valid, that didn't change the fact that it was the worst mistake I'd ever made. On top of that, I didn't even learn from it.

Four

A couple months later, I ran into a childhood friend and decided to try the love thing again. Because I'd known him for so long, since elementary school, I figured that I could trust him. After dating for about four months, I moved in with him. He played the role of stepdad to my son and everything. Lo and behold, I ended up pregnant again. As afraid as I was of having another child, I also feared ending up with another broken heart. Because I was pregnant, I prayed that God would show me signs to help me protect my heart.

Once he found out that I was pregnant, it seemed like he started taking control of me. He thought that because I was pregnant with his child I wasn't going anywhere. Little did he know, I never allowed anyone to take control of me. Although I was no longer feeling the relationship, I kept the baby anyway. A couple weeks later, we started arguing and physically fighting. I was a rough one, so it was really me who couldn't keep my hands off of him.

Thankfully, my brother had taught me a lot, so I knew every game that a man could play, including the one that was being played on me. I found out that he'd cheated on me one night after we fought. He tried to deny it, but the girl had sent me all of the evidence that I needed, including coming over to the house. She was his so called "best friend." When she came in, she grabbed his stuff and left. She later texted me, stating that they'd had sex. Initially, he denied it, but later confessed. I hated him. I regretted trusting him because he wasn't the same person I knew as a child.

I packed my stuff and ran back to my mother's house. As always, my mother had my back. I did a lot of praying around this time. I didn't want to bring another child into the world under those circumstances. I wasn't stable and had no help. Me and the child's father just wasn't seeing eye to eye. I didn't want to get an abortion, but felt that I had no better alternative. I ran to the clinic a second time. That time, I felt everything—physically and emotionally. As the procedure took place, I laid there on the hospital bed bargaining with God. *"If you bring me through this one, I promise not to open my legs again."*

After the procedure, I began to cry. I was really at the point of giving up on life. It wasn't worth it anymore. I also acknowledged that I was doing it to myself. I couldn't keep looking for love in the places that I was. I started to understand that God was putting me through a test. I failed every time I met a new guy. I was explaining this, along with my other problems, to my male friend. He'd been there for me when I was down, so I referred to him as my brother. Nights of venting, drinking, and smoking led to us having sex. Remember: I'd not long ago promised God that I'd stop opening my legs. I was upset, disappointed, and disgusted with myself. I'd just gotten an abortion, yet I didn't learn from it. Once again, I was taking God for granted.

I was still going to church, however. Three years into my membership, I started seeking God more and running from my sins and problems. I believed more in God, realizing that the more focused I was on Him, the more He showed Himself in my life. It also became clear that I wouldn't change until I knew God's purpose for my life. Because I didn't, I still backtracked. I kept going back to sin. I knew that God had a reason for everything that I was going through, but I couldn't see it or understand it.

Experience taught me that the devil shows up when I'm doing well. All of my praying and crying wasn't seeming to work. I was losing jobs back to back. I couldn't finish school. Life was getting worse every day, but I maintained my faith through it all. My tragedies didn't stop me from praying every night or trying harder to live right. I continued to get back up, dust myself off, and recharge my determination to live in alignment with God's word.

One day, my apostle spoke over my life. The word he spoke stayed in my heart. At this point, I was four years into my membership at the church and completely focused. I let God take control of my life. I began doing my part of not only going to church, but inviting others to come with me. One particular instance, I invited someone very close to me. During this time, I found out that she was raped by the man who had been my pastor when I was a little girl. Finding out something like that had me questioning how something like that could happen. *How can a pastor rape one of his members?* I couldn't believe it.

She shared that testimony and later joined the church. That made me see the light. Life is full of both pain and joy. You have to choose which road to take. Life actually isn't that hard; it's what you make it. I was set on improving my life, so I became more active in the church. I also wanted the education that I'd never received. I was focused on my goals and success. I'd never had that much peace and happiness in my life. I decided to take an even bigger step at the church and began taking classes to become ordained. Evangelizing to save unsaved souls was (and still is) my passion. I finally had my answer to why. Why me? Why had God taken me through all that? It was to make me strong. He was preparing me to do His work here on earth. That clarity was everything for me! I was more loyal to the church and living a life that I was proud of. Studying the Bible and staying connected to God was all I wanted. But remember, every time I do good, evil shows up. For me, that's usually in the form of a man. Sure enough, months later, I met a man. The flip side though was that he was a man of God.

He visited my church after one week of dating. I loved the fact that he was taking things very slowly. Two months into the relationship and everything was still good. I was all smiles. Oh, how he lit up my day! He treated me like a queen. I'd wake up to good morning texts, encouraging texts to get me through the day, and other little things that counted. Finding love in all the wrong places no longer applied to me. I'd finally met a man who understood and respected my wishes and goals in life. The way he made me smile, his sense of humor, and our bond was second to none.

After a few more weeks of dating, we went out and had a nice time. We got a room at a hotel and though he respected that I wanted to save myself, I slipped up and had sex with him that night. We both felt really bad about it. But instead of continuing down that path, I told him that I wasn't having sex again until I got married. Though he understood and agreed, it didn't make me feel any less bad about what I'd done. I sat in my room one day and cried out to God that I wasn't getting anywhere in life. I continued to disappoint God, my saver, the one who loved me in spite of all my wrongdoing, the who woke me up everyday, gave His only son for us, had my back when no one else did, etc. I could go on and on about the greatness of God, but how could I keep taking him for granted? I was wasting time. I had to make a decision. It was either God or Satan. I chose God because it wasn't Satan who was keeping me alive.

I also chose to continue spending time with my friend. I'd never spent so much time with a man, including spending the night, without having sex with him. That was all new to me. It also demonstrated the deliverance from my biggest weakness, which was my addiction to sex. Though we didn't have sex anymore, that didn't hinder our relationship. For instance, not long afterwards, he invited me and my son to the circus. We had a wonderful time. He did things that I'd never done with any other man, but in a good way. I was still afraid to trust or love another man again, however. I just wanted to keep having a good time. Love complicated things.

Five

2014 was my year of deliverance. Prayer comes before anything I do now, and I always seek to put God first, trusting and believing in Him that everything will be okay. Though I was good in the relationship department, I still struggled with my professional goals. I was back to filling out applications and trying to get my GED, but I only ended up back in the place of confusion. I was doing the best I could in serving God—no sex, drugs, clubbing, or anything—but it seemed like nothing was going right in my life. When stuck in sin, it seemed like blessings were handed to me. Now that I was focused, it was hard to see a blessing.

The Pages Haven't Run Out Yet

I was back to crying at night to release some pain. I never doubted that the God I serve is amazing, but I'm still human and can't help but cry sometimes. I concluded that God was trying to teach me patience. That if I kept my mind focused on God, my success would come. Then, on April 11th, my old job called and offered me the position of a manager. I took it. Not long after, Job Corp called with an opportunity to finish the program. *God is so good!* I stayed focused and look what happened! My birthday is also in April, so things were looking good for my new year of life.

My boo had plans for me. On the 13th, he surprised me and took me to see the Bible play. That was the best birthday gift ever. The next day, my actual birthday, he took me to dinner then dropped me off. The day didn't end as well as it started because I hadn't heard from him at all that night. I didn't have time to be worrying about why he was mad though, so I moved on.

On April 17th, I went to church for communion and the service went so well! After church, me and a friend had planned to go to the casino. Before going, we said a prayer. We ended up not being able to go because she didn't have her ID. I saw it as God intercepting. So we went back to her house, sat down, and talked about God. I showed her the book that I'd been writing (this one), and she shared how it touched her in many ways. I didn't foresee my story delivering her, but it did. She went on to tell me some things that I didn't know she'd been going through. We hadn't talked in a while, but God separated us for a reason. Now back together, we were both on the right track!

God has His ways of doing things. It's just so amazing how He turned us around that night. That night helped me to further understand my vision and purpose here on earth. It's to serve young women out here and help bring them back to Christ. In doing so, I couldn't keep living in the past and reminding myself about the people who hurt or betrayed me. Just as Jesus was sent to save us, he couldn't worry about the people who were going to betray him. If he focused on them, he wouldn't have been able to do what God sent him to do. We have to have the same mindset. Love the ones who do us wrong. At the end of the day, God placed us here to be an example of the body of Christ. There are souls that need to be saved. People need to know the gospel of Christ; God is still able and Jesus is the son of God. He who believes in Jesus Christ shall live and not die.

On April 23rd at exactly one in the morning, the devil showed up. My friend came to pick me up. We were chilling and having a good time, then he asked to have sex. Temptation was strong, so I began to pray. After prayer, I had my strength back. A week later, my apostle spoke over me. "If he wants to marry you, he will wait." That word helped me to stand my ground. If I expected others to respect my standards, then I had to respect them first. And if he couldn't, then he wasn't worth having me. I realized then that fighting temptation wasn't going to get any easier. It'd get harder, knowing that the devil is always present when you're on the right track. I thought about how far I'd come and how it wasn't worth going back. Giving in only temporarily satisfies our flesh.

I'm more interested in feeding my spirit. My testimony isn't just for me. It's for someone else. I hold tight by reminding myself that I've come too far to go back. I reminded my friend that I'd let that sin go. God can only deliver me from it if I'm willing to let it happen. He replies that it's okay and that he has no choice but to respect it, and then goes on to say, "That's a tough one, the fact that we're not on the same page." At that point, I'm leaning on the side of just walking away. Since I didn't want to end up backtracking, I decided to step away from the dating scene and focus on my mission instead.

Watch how the devil works...

Six

On May 15th, my very first love texted me, asking me to pray hard for him. We'd never fully lost contact with one another considering that he and my brother were friends, but we hadn't talked for about four or five months straight before this text. I didn't understand why, out of the blue, he texted me that. I questioned if it was God or the devil. Just when I'd decided to focus on me, here comes my first love out of nowhere. I called him to find out what was going on and learned that he was in a serious situation. I began praying for him. He asked me to come to church with him for his father's 32nd year anniversary. I agreed. After spending time together that day, he noted how I'd been there for him all these years and how much of a woman of God I'd become. He also stated that he no longer wanted to take me for granted and that he was ready to change. He was ready to fulfill his purpose here on earth. Like me, he was tired of the devil taking control of him.

I've always had a weak spot for him, and that fact he wanted to get right with God made me want to help him. I knew he would one day come back to God, but I didn't think I would fall back in love with him again. We started hanging out more. His family would tell me how much they've missed me and how much I was meant to be in his life. Since we were both on the same spiritual page, we decided to try the relationship thing again. This time, we were going to do it the right way: no sex before marriage and we'd keep God first in everything.

He still had a problem with drinking, and I really disliked the fact he struggled with this sin. I understand that change doesn't happen overnight, so I was willing to help him through it. About a month later, he shouted for the first time in church. *God is good!* More and more, I was beginning to understand my purpose. I'd been celibate for about eight months when he started to bring up sex. He respected me enough not to ask me, but he did say that he wished we were able to have sex one more time before he went celibate. I felt bad for him, so we planned to do it one last time. After that, we'd wait until we got married. We were going to get the hotel on August 11th. Until then, we had to fight temptation.

My apostle called me and told me that I was scheduled to preach my first sermon on July 25th. I was so scared, but knew I had to stay focused, so I cut a lot of people off. My boyfriend was by my side the whole month, including times of fasting and prayer. In addition to coming to church with me, he even met with my apostle. July 25th arrived and everyone but my father was present, which upset me.

He'd gotten out of prison in 2009. While he was locked up, we'd formed somewhat of a relationship. I'd write him and tell him how I was feeling, especially when I was down. He'd always write back and say things to keep me encouraged. I assumed that when he got out, we'd continue to build on what we'd started. Needless to say, it didn't happen.

Though he wasn't there, other family members were, including my boyfriend, mother, stepfather, and other family members. So I was satisfied. The title of my sermon was "Do you know your purpose?" I set the church on fire! Afterwards, I received my certificate as a minister\evangelist, which meant that I could legitimately preach and teach the gospel of Jesus Christ. This filled me with so much joy and peace, but I was still a little bothered by the fact that my father didn't show up.

Not long after, the devil came creeping. My boyfriend got into an accident on his bike. That same night, I found out that not only was he still drinking, but that he had been with a girl. His father called me at two in the morning, and we rushed to the hospital to see if he was okay. He apologized and confessed that he was still suffering with the sin of drinking. I forgave him and we tried to work it out with more prayer. Weeks passed, and he went back to doing the same things. It was really distracting at that point. August arrived, and we were getting close to the date they we set aside to have sex. I began regretting even agreeing to it. I'd begun noticing how much higher I tend to put other's feelings before my own. Too often am I loyal to people who take me for granted. So I called him and told him that it was off.

Watch how God worked it out...

Weeks later, he called me to come over. While waiting for him to pick me up, I overheard him on the phone and found out that he'd cheated on me again. I hurt, but I refused to let it take me back. I broke up with him. I eventually forgave him, but I had a lot of bitterness towards him. I couldn't believe he would cheat on me again after I'd given him another chance. He texted and called to say how hurt and upset he was with himself because he'd lost me again and knew I wasn't taking him back again. He was right. I'd lost all trust and respect for him.

I then realized that I had to endure a season of loneliness, and deservingly so. I'd been disobedient, considering the fact that my apostle told me to take it slow. I didn't, and the consequence was a broken heart. He and I are still good friends. No grudges. I still pray for his deliverance, but I've moved on. I needed to be free from it all! I had to learn to fully love myself before I loved anyone else, and a season of being single is just what I needed.

Seven

I applied for a job at the Gaylord again and was scheduled for an interview on August 12th, the day after I'd planned to have sex. Goes to show that everything happens for a reason. We broke up just in time. I would have missed my blessing from backtracking. The first part of my interview went well. During the second part, I received a call from my doctor saying that I had an STD that could lead to cancer. I hadn't had sex in over eight months and was okay before that call, so I didn't understand. On top of that, I received this call during my interview. I knew it had to be the devil trying to distract me. I blocked it all out and stayed focused. On the way home from the interview, the job called and asked me to come back. I did, and they offered me a higher position, paying even more money. God favored me because in the midst of getting bad news, I didn't lose faith.

Everything was going well. I got the job that I'd been praying for since forever. All it took was obedience, patience, faith, and focus. *God is so good!* On September 19th, I went back to the doctor to get tested again. The following Sunday, during church, my apostle touched my stomach and said that it was gone. A week later, my doctor called to say that the test results came back negative for all infections and diseases, including cancer. I was so overjoyed, I didn't know what to do with myself. Not only was a God a healer, but a provider as well. I was set to start my new job on October 9th.

There was only one thing left for me to do to fully clear my heart of all resentment and anger, including the hate towards my mother. We sat down and had a long talk one night. During that conversation, I found out that my mother never knew about me being molested. My aunt had never told her. And come to find out, molestation runs on my father's side of the family. Now I was even more devastated. I'd been angry for all that time, yet my mother didn't even know. Now I was on a journey for answers!

I wanted to know where this family curse of being molested came from and where it began.

I asked God to give me an answer. Ever since I asked God, my answer began being thrown in my face. I found out where it started, and I couldn't believe my ears. This was a life shocking situation! After my source told me where it started, I wanted to go directly to the two who started it, but I promised the person who told me that I wouldn't tell a soul. So I went to God: "Lord, I don't know when this will be revealed, but I do know it will hurt a lot of people." I'm still in shock about it, but I thank God I have matured so I know how to handle it.

Weeks later, my favorite little cousin came over to my house after a long night out for some girl talk. We began to talk about God and our goals in life. Being as though she looks up to me, I try my best to stay positive around her and to be a good example. So far I have been doing a great job at that. We discussed my book and I shared some things with

The Pages Haven't Run Out Yet

her. That conversation led to her telling me that she was also molested by a family member. At that point, I was like WOW! She told me the whole story from beginning to end. The entire time, I sat there in shock. I couldn't believe it. I was finding out more and more about my dad's side of the family curse. I allowed her to vent that night because I knew how she felt. I've been there. I was so glad she stayed a night so she was able to go to church with me Sunday.

Not long after that, my oldest cousin and her mother got into a big fight. I reached out to her to find out what happened. She began to cry out to me about how much I have motivated her to do better. I was unaware that she was watching my change and had been seeking God since I preached my first sermon. That touched my heart in a special way, knowing my change in life motivated her to do better. She shared how her stepfather molested her for years.

She explained that her mother—the aunt I'd told about me being molested—knew, but didn't do anything about it. Sound familiar? I then realized that the family curse had a lot to do with secrets.

That made me very angry, however, I maintained my composure. After all, it was what I'd asked for. I asked the question and God was revealing the answer. After learning her story, I understood why her life went the way it did. Everyone used to judge her and the decisions she made in life, but no one knew what she went through. I went through the same thing with finding love in the wrong places. Sometimes we can be judgmental but not know the reason behind someone's actions. Never judge a book by its cover.

From that night on, I cried out to God on her behalf. But for some odd reason, after hearing all of this, it made me think about my first love. I guess because we'd grown a bond. I entrusted him with the molestations. So I got use to venting to him. My love for him is still unconditional. Sometimes I feel like I can still build a future with him, but my standards sometimes makes my pride stand high. It's hard to hide when my heart is crying out louder than my pride. They say you never forget your first true love, but I'll never forget my first heartbreak either. Is it wrong to say I still love him when I fear trusting him? My spirit speaks to me, my mind sometimes overthinks, my flesh fights my soul, yet I have control.

God, please lead and protect me from my emotions before I end up down the same road of destruction. I want to be free from the thought of loving him. I want to be free from the thought of being hurt by him. They say forgiveness is best for letting go of the past. Is it safe to still feel the way I feel about him? Is it a sign of still being deeply in love with him? Secretly I'm thinking of him, but God I know you have a plan bigger than my emotions and my pain. I'm patiently waiting for my king that you will soon send. Yet I still ask, is it safe to love him?

All this crying and talking to God made me realize that I'd released the bitterness that I held after he hurt me a second time. I felt good after all of that crying. I texted him to get closure on the relationship so I could really move on. I now have no one to vent to but my mother about this journey of finding my answer. However, there are times she's unavailable, so I'm learning to vent to and rely on God more and more. Planting those seeds of trust in God bears amazing fruit.

I started my job at the Gaylord. Everything was going well. I'd never felt so happy with a job in my whole life. I finally felt in place with my life. No more relationship problems. I was focused on my career and my son. I met new friends on the job. One has been coming to church with me. Though we often talk about God, I try not to minister too much on the job. Me and one of my managers always have conversation about church. One of these conversation resulted in one of the leads getting bothered by it.

"Hey, don't talk about God so much. You might offend someone," she said.

"That's why we are having this conversation at lunch," I answered.

Ever since that day, my lead has been acting funny towards me. I continue coming to work and minding my business. I didn't like the vibe I started to get from her, so I kept my distance which is hard because she is the lead of the office. My days at work started to get a little weird. I tried not to focus on that too much though. I'd rather focus on the good like my developing relationship with my father. I occasionally still think about the fact that he missed my first sermon. I have yet to find out why he wasn't there. I try not to linger on the past too much because I want to move forward with him, but it's difficult sometimes. I believe he didn't spend time with us when he got out because he was so quick to get remarried and that his wife played a big part in his absence in his kids' lives.

We've grown closer though. We've been hanging out every day and having daughter and daddy dates. He takes me to work and picks me up. All I ever wanted was a relationship with my dad. Long conversations with him have taught me how to open up to him more. This is the most time I have spent with him since he's been home from jail. He's begun sharing his mistakes and the reasons why he hasn't been there like he'd promised. Out of all my siblings, I'm the only one to have forgiven him. In spite of his dark secrets, I love him the same. I have never felt so much joy and happiness in my life as I have in the past two months.

But just when I think everything is good, the devil finds a ways to show up to steal my happiness. For instance, I'd just gotten to work one day when my manager told me that she was sending me home. I asked her what was going on and she told me it has something to do with accounting. So I went home. Later on that day, I found out that my lead—the same one who told me to stop talking about God so much—was making complaints, saying I did things I hadn't done. I immediately recognized it as an attack of the enemy. I got straight down on my knees and I cried out to God because I didn't understand why my blessing was being taken from me. I knew to trust God, but I'm still human and still had my doubts. I just didn't understand. It was like once I received it, it was taken from me. I didn't do anything different; I stayed obedient and paid my tithes. Yet there I was feeling the same pain as when I first got my heart broken. I told myself I didn't want to feel that pain again, but that's exactly what it felt like.

I sit here and cry as I write this. Not out of anger, but pain and joy. Through all of this, I still trust God. Just because one blessing was taken, I look back on my life and I have more than enough to be grateful for. We tend to get stuck on and blinded by material things. So when God (seemingly) stops blessing us, we turn our backs and begin to

The Pages Haven't Run Out Yet

question Him. I didn't. Not this time; I kept my faith. Honestly, Jesus dying on the cross is the best blessing I could ever ask for.

I called my apostle the same day they sent me home. He told me not to worry and that he would pray on my behalf. After talking to him, I called my grandmother to get her opinion on things. She said the same thing, and I found that comforting. Furthermore, my apostle checked on me every day to see if I heard anything from the job. He has been more than my apostle over the years. He has been more like a dad to me. Having a leader that really cares about his people is a blessing by itself. I told him I still hadn't heard a word. He replied with encouragement. I haven't lost my faith, nor have I lost my trust. I believe whatever God is doing. I learned not to question him. If I say I trust him then why question his decisions? I just have to be patient and see what happens from here.

I thank God for spiritual people in my life. Two very special people I have, I call them my sisters in Christ. One of them was there for me when I was stuck in darkness. She was there to encourage me. Every time I slipped and fell, she picked me right up. She was my ride to the abortion clinic when I went through that rough time. She was my shoulder to cry on and my ear to vent to about my crazy relationships. She held all my secrets and was one of the first people I learned to trust at the church.

The other one was my motivation to get where I'm at in Christ today. When I first met her, she was so kind. Like me, she was fighting flesh to get to Christ. When I saw her take her first step at our church by becoming an evangelist, I began to take mine. When she got ordained, it made me thirst for God more. When I'm down and my flesh seems to sneak up, she's always a phone call away. She's more like my strength when I'm weak. She always knows what to say and when to say it to get me back on track. I can talk to her about anything without her judging me or looking down on me. She has truly been my partner in Christ. Everyone needs that spiritual sister.

I also vented to her about the job and everything else that was going on, and as always, she was right by my side. I know you're probably wondering what happened to my close friends. Well, after preaching my first sermon, I learned you have to let go of some people to move forward. I found out things about them that hurt me, and I was so tired of being stabbed in my back and being hurt by people. I still love them the same, but I had to let go of my old habits, including them, in order to change.

Eight

My father was a prophet and a preacher. Even though he was stuck in his flesh, he was still a man of God. He'd prophesied when he named me. My name would be the start of my destiny. I'd have the free and unmerited favor of God as manifested in the salvation of sinners and the bestowal of blessings. My purpose began the day I was born, and my father being imprisoned was a part of my destiny. He designed me to be strong and bold. The storms of my life were to build me up for my ministry.

When you have a calling over your life, it comes with a storm and lessons to learn from it. My father being sent to jail was stage one. Being molested was stage two. Finding love in the wrong place was stage three.

If we pay close attention, everything happens in stages. God takes us through a process before He births what He called you to do. Through every stage, I learned something different. Everything has a purpose. When I was molested, for example, it caused me to go hunting for love. As I matured, I realized that I had to start loving myself. I learned how to respect my body more. God didn't allow it to happen to harm me. He used it to help me. Sounds crazy, right? It's true though. Being molested helped me grow into the woman I am today. It positioned me to be able to help other women more effectively.

Finding love in the wrong places made me seek God more. Sometimes God allows us to live in the dark so that we'll *want* the light. Suffering from heartache made me pray more. The more the devil let me down, the more I sought God. I've always been searching for the light. I was called to be an evangelist to preach the gospel of God. With that type of calling over your life comes a journey of trials and tribulation.

God delivers you through the hard parts of life to birth your purpose. Everything you go through builds your purpose. If you look back on the good and the bad—all the struggle, pain, hurt, and tears—then you'll see your purpose. What God puts you through is your purpose. When God forgives you for your sins, He makes you a new creature, which means you are a new person. You have a new due date. You can start off clean. No sin, no nothing, just like Jesus did. If God hasn't given you your death date yet, it's time to know your purpose. Stop looking at the devil's purpose. Look at your testimony and ask God to start giving you understanding of your purpose.

Now that I have my answer, I'm in the process of seeing that this curse is broken. From my understanding, a generational curse or family curse can only be broken through repentance, prayer, deliverance, and confessing. Curses come from demonic spirits. The Bible mentions "generational curses" in several places, including Exodus 20:5 and 34:7, Numbers 14:18, and Deuteronomy 5:9. God warns that He is "a jealous God, punishing the children for the sin of the fathers to the third and fourth generation of those who hate me." Numbers

14:18 declares that "the LORD is slow to anger and abounding in steadfast love, forgiving iniquity and transgression, but he will by no means clear the guilty, visiting the iniquity of the fathers on the children, to the third and the fourth generation."

Let's say your father has a drug addiction and he gets married. He never breaks his addiction, gets married, and has kids. His kids are now growing up, watching the negativity of his addiction, which now plays a part of their life. They begin feeding off of his energy which are the spirits that he's fighting. The father's drug addiction causes him to abuse both his wife and his children—verbally, physically, and/or sexually. As a result of this kind of severe transgression against the Lord, demons will be allowed to come in and attach themselves to the father.

Once the demons settle, they will then see which of the children they can target. They will try to persuade one or more of the children to become a drug addict themselves just like their father was. As a result of this kind of direct demonic influence that will start early on in their lives, some of these children will end up becoming drug addicts themselves once they are old enough to leave their home and move into their own marriages. They end up repeating some of the same dysfunctional behaviors as their father. They then have their own children. Those children watch and experience their dysfunctional behavior, and grow up with the same demonic influence as their parent, leaving to become alcoholics (or drug addicts) themselves. The cycle keeps repeating itself further down the bloodline of these families.

Through my studies, I've learned that the curse won't be stop until the head person breaks it. My two family members who started this curse along with the drug abusing and molestations are the cause of our generation curses. In order to stop it, the secrets have to be told. Someone will have to come forth and stop this dysfunctional behavior. Until then, I will continue on my journey. I found the answers I have been searching for. My next question is when it will be revealed.

I know the secret, but I promised I wouldn't tell.

Sometimes I feel like it's not my place to tell it. After all, she only told me because she trusted me with it.

God doesn't move in mess, so I know I'm not the one who's supposed to come forth and tell it. I just pray that they will step up so that this cycle can be stopped. I fear for my son. I don't want it to continue in his generation, so I do everything in my power to stay positive and spiritual around him. The Bible say in Proverbs 22:6, "Train up a child in the way he should go,

And when he is old he will not depart from it."

Conclusion

Life has been a journey,
but the pages haven't run out yet.

Throughout all of my experiences, God never left my side, even when I turned back on Him. I'm working and am very active in the church. I received my certificate to evangelize and preach the gospel, thus fulfilling my purpose. I'm blessed and very happy with my life. I still have some questions that need to be answered and secrets that need to be told. I'm on a new journey for God and for finding the answers to my questions.

You can't move forward if you're still holding on to old people and things. Change starts with cutting people and old habits off. Yes, it's hard. Deliverance doesn't happen overnight. It's a process. Yes, it hurts, but that's the process of changing and becoming better. It took me five years after giving myself back to Christ to get to my full deliverance and to get where I'm at today—all because I didn't want to let go of people and my old habits. How can you get delivered from something if you're not willing to let it go? When I finally started to separate myself from people and habits like drinking, smoking, clubbing, and sex, I realized my change was coming quicker. I could no longer be around people who were still doing those things. I had to find positive people to be around so that my deliverance could take place. God gives us a free will to choose darkness or light. We can either do right by Him or be against Him. It's your choice.

If we really take a look at our lives, the decisions we make play a big part. Life is about making the right choices. In my situation, I was tired of living in darkness, allowing the devil to take control. I wasn't getting far at all. I realized I was stuck in the same place and wasn't accomplishing anything. Sin might please my flesh for a moment, but it was affecting my life in a more long-term way. I was taking myself down a road of death and not eternal life. If I can take back the stuff I did, I would. But I can't, so I thank God for loving me past every sin and creating me to be new. My sins turned into my testimony. They allowed me to grow into a mature woman of God. And that's only because I didn't stay in my sin. I learned from them and allowed God to deliver me from them. Yes, it took me five years of being with my church for me to get delivered from my addiction, but that's because I took that long to say yes to God's will. I'm more focused on my goals and success. I'm an evangelist/minister in training, and there is more to this story. My journey does not end here.

I thank God for my deliverance!

My thirst for God is *unbelievable*. I'm learning more about life and the whole meaning of life. There's more to it than what we think. God's plan is bigger than what we can imagine. My apostle teaches us the roots of things, or should I say he goes *deep*. For example, it's 24 hours in a day for us, but 12 hours in a day for Jews. Darkness equals the beginning which is light, and light equals the end which is day. Evening and morning were the first days: 6PM to 6AM. So if we look at it in Jews' time, there are 12 hours in a day. We're so stuck on our time when God is moving in a whole different time, prophetic time. I also learned the prayer times which are 3AM and 3PM.

It's important to be connected to the right church. Improper teaching will have you bound and lost in this world. Why be under a leader and see no change in your life? If it wasn't for God allowing me to meet this great man of God, I wouldn't understand life the way I do. I would still be stuck in darkness. He helps me look at life a different way. I have a better understanding of church and God. It's not about tradition. I now know the reasons for what I do in church. I'm not just doing it because I grew up around it. Christians tend to play church but not know the meaning behind praise, prayer, or worship. Being under this ministry, however, I have learned the reasons. I've always learned that I no longer have to worry about my son and his safety. With God on my side, I won't fail. I still worry for the rest of my cousins, aunts, and their kids though because the curse still plays a big part in their life. This curse must be broken. The devil will no longer have a hold on my family.

Besides all of that, I'm happy with my life. I will be applying for school in February of 2015. My son is now in school, so I can work towards my success. My goals in life are set. Just look how God transformed my life. I'm still single. It's been ten months since I've been celibate, but I do talk back to my friend – the man of God I have mentioned before. Nothing serious, just friends. By the end of 2015, I will be where I want to be in life. God will show up and show out. Just watch how my life turns out.

To be continued...

A New Journey

Five Steps to Help You Begin Your Journey to Hope and Deliverance

1. Find a home church:

The Universal Church derives its definition from the baptizing ministry of the Holy Spirit. "By one Spirit we are all baptized into one body." (1 Corinthians 12:13)

2. Get saved:

Salvation is deliverance from danger or suffering. To save is to deliver or protect. The word carries the idea of victory, health, or preservation. Sometimes the Bible uses the words saved or salvation to refer to temporal, physical deliverance, such as Paul's deliverance from prison (Philippians 1:19).

3. Rededicate yourself:

Rededicating your life to Christ is a popular concept in modern Christian culture. It's a decision made by a Christian who has fallen away from the practices of Christianity to turn back to Christ and strive to follow Him more completely. The act of suddenly returning to Christ is spoken of indirectly in Galatians 6:1.

4. Worship:

God, in all of His glory, chooses to respond to us through our worship. This is the promise—that when we worship God with love and extreme submission, God will come and commune with us. Psalm 96:13 declares, "Before the Lord: for he cometh, for he cometh to judge the earth: he shall judge the world with righteousness, and the people with his truth." As best stated by Christianity Today:

"The other benefits that we tend to expect because we lift up our feeble hands and shout with our weak voices are worthless if our hearts are not right with God. Thus, my sisters and brothers, when we offer God our true worship, we are inviting him to inspect our hearts for anything that is not like him. This is the promise of worship—we can be transformed into God's likeness because he will reveal the truth about the condition of our hearts as we worship him."

5. Get Delivered:

While believers are delivered once for all time from eternal punishment, we are also delivered from the trials of this life (2 Peter 2:9).

Sometimes that deliverance is God simply walking through the trials by our side, comforting and encouraging us through them as He uses them to mature us in the faith. God is faithful; He will not let you be tempted beyond what you can bear. But when you are tempted, He will also provide a way out so that you can stand up under it" (1 Corinthians 10:13).

About the Author

Evangelist Grace Garnett helps people who struggle in identifying the purpose of their traumatic pasts. Through her own testimony in her book, *The Pages Haven't Run Out Yet* she demonstrates that your past was planted to build your purpose.

Garnett's primary mission is leaving this earth empty of everything God has called her to do while helping others do the same. In addition to ministering and mothering her son, Jabriel, Garnett also has a passion for traveling, dancing and painting, which has led to her winning the Job Corp Best Painter Award in 2009.

To learn more, visit: **www.About.Me/GraceGarnett**

 @evangelist_grace   /msevangelistgrace

www.ingramcontent.com/pod-product-compliance
Lightning Source LLC
Chambersburg PA
CBHW052114070526
44584CB00017B/2479